magic STORY STARTERS

Linda Polon

Scott, Foresman and Company
Glenview, Illinois   London

 **Good Year Books**

are available for preschool through grade 12 and for
every basic curriculum subject plus many enrichment
areas. For more Good Year Books, contact your local
bookseller or educational dealer. For a complete
catalog with information about other Good Year Books,
please write:

Good Year Books
Department GYB
1900 East Lake Avenue
Glenview, Illinois 60025

ISBN 0-673-18561-3

5 6-MAL-91 90 89

INTRODUCTION

This book is designed to stir up the creativity in your students, inspiring them to think and write freely. The most reluctant, stubborn students will find themselves enjoying the activities in this book. The more eager writers in your class will find the lessons challenging enough to stimulate their creative abilities.

The purpose of this book is to give a variety of writing experiences. The activities proceed from the simple to the more difficult. The activities can be taken out of order depending on your students' abilities.

The book is divided into five parts. In the first part (Words, Words), words are given to help children write their stories. Not all the words to the story are supplied. The children have to come up with some of their own words. In the second part (Finishing Touches), the beginning sentence of a story is given and children write the rest of the story. For the third part (Starts and Stops), children write the beginning and ending to a story after the middle part is given. In the fourth part (Giant Steps), the ending of the story is given and children write the beginning and the middle part of the story. In the fifth part (The Big Picture), children write a complete story after looking at a picture. This last section of activities allows both the students and teacher to assess student growth. Also, the teacher can note if a student needs more practice in writing and could then redirect the student to a story section covering the student's deficient needs.

To aide the children in writing stories, pictures are on each page to inspire their thoughts, ideas and ignite their creativity.

I hope your students enjoy working in this book as much as I did writing it.

DEDICATION

To Laurie Wolff, a loving sister and best friend

To Joan Horner, a caring friend

To Bob Dorsey, my loving husband

To Caren Scott, a wonderful friend

To Brooke Barton for her guidance and love for the illustration on page 35

To my marvelous, supportive parents, Hal and Edie Wolff

TABLE OF CONTENTS

WORDS, WORDS

Write a story about the pictures. Use the words below to help you write your story. Do not forget to write a title.

princess   prince   frog   crown   change

kiss   is   happy   going   there

_____

_____

_____

_____

_____

_____

Words, Words

Name _____

Date _____

Write a story about the picture. Use the words below to help you write your story. Do not forget to write a title.

monsters	mean	unhappy	big	claws
ugly	alike	look	they	fat	eyes

_____

_____

_____

_____

_____

_____

WORDS, WORDS

Write a story about the picture. Use the words below to help you write your story. Do not forget to write a title.

man   funny   wonder   tape measure   sack

mystery   inside   small   surprise

_____

_____

_____

_____

_____

_____

Words, Words

Write a story about the pictures. Use the words below to help you write your story. Do not forget to write a title.

dad   girl   present   large   gift   box

ribbon   happy   surprise   the   smiling

_____

_____

_____

_____

_____

_____

_____

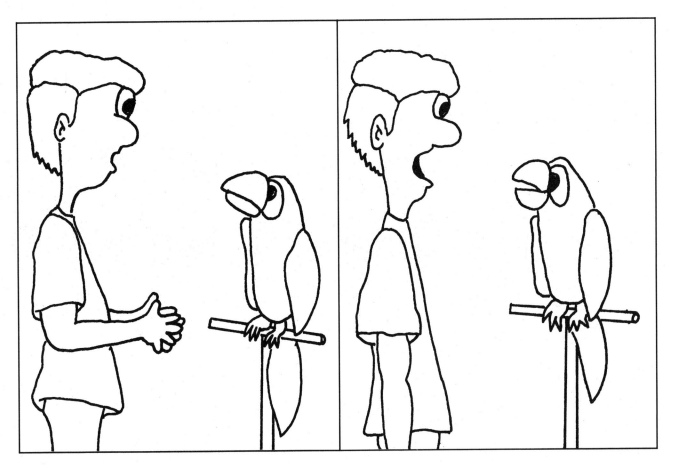

Write a story about the pictures. Use the words below to help you write your story. Do not forget to write a title.

boy   parrot   talking   stand   have

words   the   funny   conversation

_____

_____

_____

_____

_____

_____

_____

5

WORDS, WORDS

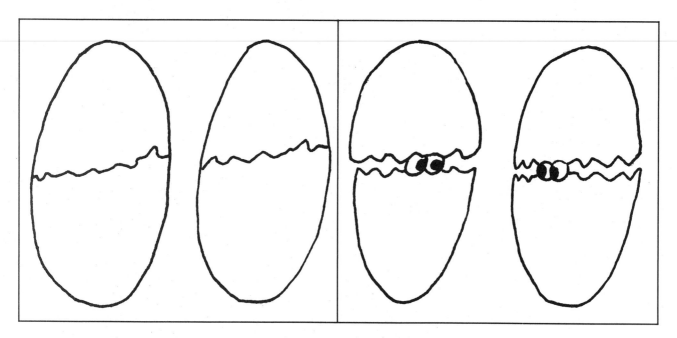

Write a story about the pictures. Use the words below to help you write your story. Do not forget to write a title.

large	eggs	two	shell	crack	eyes	there
are	look	the	black	talk	each	other

_____

_____

_____

_____

_____

_____

_____

_____

_____

WORDS, WORDS

Name _____

Date _____

Write a story about the picture. Use the words below to help you write your story. Do not forget to write a title.

boy   girl   same   walk   smile

surprise   street   flowers   love

_____

_____

_____

_____

_____

_____

_____

WORDS, WORDS

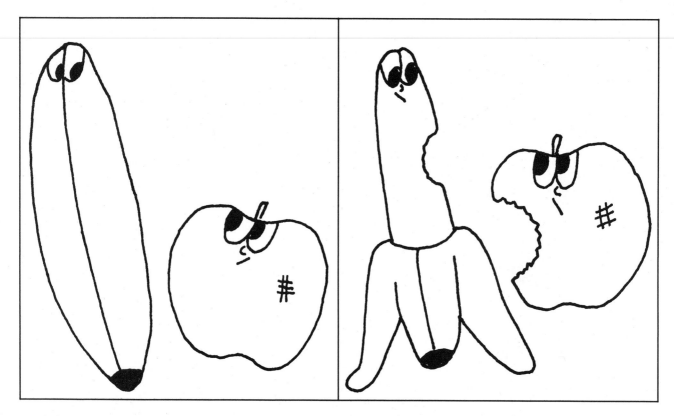

Write a story about the pictures. Use the words below to help you write your story. Do not forget to write a title.

fruit   banana   apple   scared   surprised

bite   missing   part   piece   fight

_____

_____

_____

_____

_____

_____

_____

WORDS, WORDS

Write a story about the pictures. Use the words below to help you write your story. Do not forget to write a title.

boy   girl   string   kite   paper   colors

fly   float   up   sky   disappear   yell

_____

_____

_____

_____

_____

_____

_____

FINISHING TOUCHES

Name _____

Date _____

Finish the story about the picture. Do not forget to write a title.

You hear something. You run. You turn your head and see a _____

_____

_____

_____

_____

_____

_____

_____

F INISHING TOUCHES

Finish the story about the pictures. Do not forget to write a title.

The girl mixes the liquids. Something happens. There is _____

_____

_____

_____

_____

_____

_____

_____

Finish the story about the picture. Do not forget to write a title.

The girl is skiing. Suddenly _____

_____

_____

_____

_____

_____

_____

_____

_____

_____

_____

_____

_____

_____

_____

_____

_____

Name _____

Date _____

Finish the story about the pictures. Do not forget to write a title.

Nobody will believe me, but it did happen. It all started when _____

_____

_____

_____

_____

_____

_____

_____

FINISHING TOUCHES

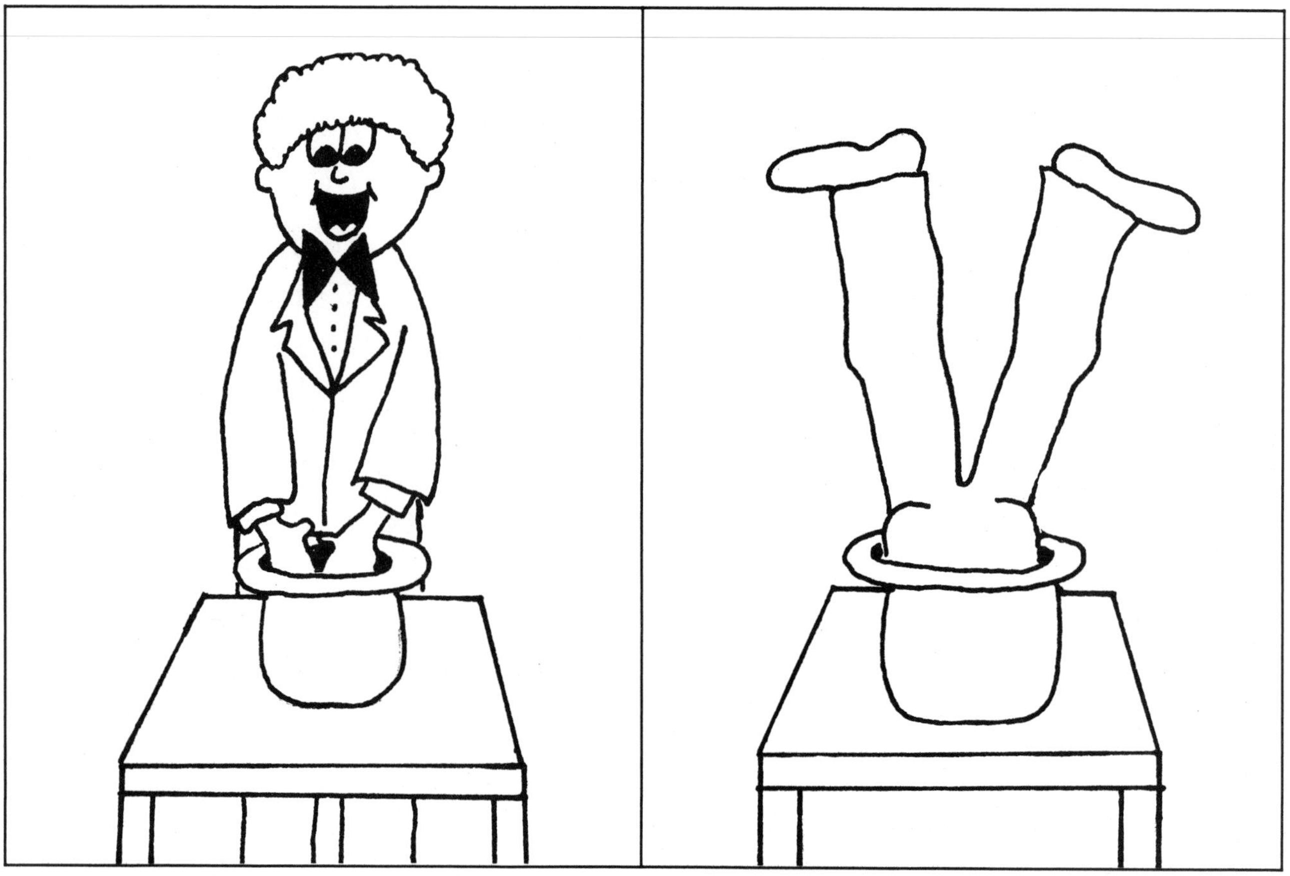

Finish the story about the pictures. Do not forget to write a title.

A magician is doing a trick. Then suddenly _____

_____

_____

_____

_____

_____

_____

_____

FINISHING TOUCHES

Name _____

Date _____

Finish the story about the picture. Do not forget to write a title.

Was I dreaming? In front of me stood a _____

_____

_____

_____

_____

_____

_____

_____

_____

Finish the story about the picture. Do not forget to write a title.

The girl drank a secret formula. In the next minute she looked like a___

_____

_____

_____

_____

_____

_____

_____

_____

FINISHING TOUCHES

Finish the story about the picture. Do not forget to write a title.

The man slipped on a banana peel, but that was only the start of

his problems. Next, he _____

_____

_____

_____

_____

_____

_____

_____

_____

_____

_____

_____

_____

_____

FINISHING TOUCHES

Name _____

Date _____

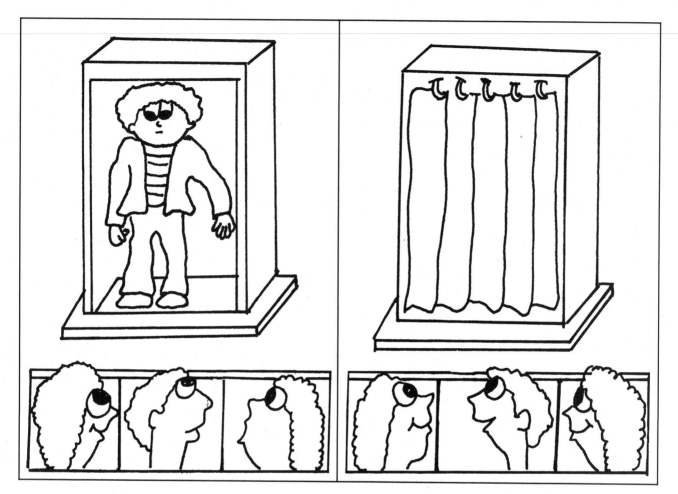

Finish the story about the pictures. Do not forget to write a title.

The boy is in a booth. The curtain closes and _____

_____

_____

_____

_____

_____

_____

STARTS AND STOPS

Write the beginning and ending of a story about the pictures. Do not forget to write a title.

_____

_____

_____

_____

_____

The two snakes looked funny. _____

_____

_____

_____

_____

Write the beginning and ending of a story about the pictures. Do not forget to write a title.

_____

_____

_____

_____

The saw goes through the box. _____

_____

_____

_____

STARTS AND STOPS

Write the beginning and ending of a story about the picture. Do not forget to write a title.

_____

_____

_____

They were about to crash. _____

_____

_____

_____

Write the beginning and ending of a story about the picture. Do not forget to write a title.

_____

_____

_____

_____

The three ghosts looked at each other. _____

_____

_____

_____

_____

_____

STARTS AND STOPS

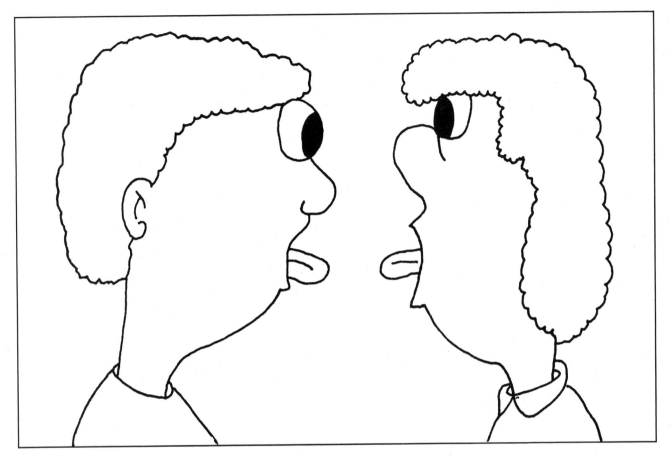

Write the beginning and ending of a story about the picture. Do not forget to write a title.

_____

_____

_____

_____

They stopped fighting for a minute. _____

_____

_____

_____

STARTS AND STOPS

Write the beginning and ending of a story about the pictures. Do not forget to write a title.

_____

_____

_____

"I am right," said one of the boys.

"NO. I am right," said the other boy.

_____

_____

_____

Sᴛᴀʀᴛꜱ ᴀɴᴅ Sᴛᴏᴘꜱ

Write the beginning and ending of a story about the picture. Do not forget to write a title.

_____

_____

_____

_____

_____

_____

_____

Both of them wiggled. _____

_____

_____

_____

_____

_____

_____

_____

Write the beginning and ending of a story about the picture. Do not forget to write a title.

_____

_____

_____

She bought something she always wanted. _____

_____

_____

_____

_____

STARTS AND STOPS

Write the beginning and ending of a story about the picture. Do not forget to write a title.

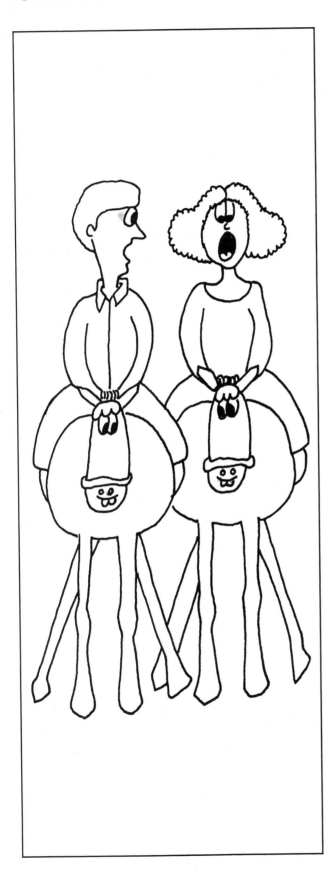

_____

_____

_____

_____

_____

_____

The horses ran faster and faster.

_____

_____

_____

_____

_____

_____

_____

GIANT STEPS

Name _____

Date _____

Read the ending of the story about the picture. Write the beginning and the middle part of the story. Do not forget to write a title.

_____

_____

_____

_____

_____

_____

_____

_____

I did it. What a race!

GIANT STEPS

Read the ending of the story about the pictures. Write the beginning
and the middle part of the story. Do not forget to write a title.

_____

_____

_____

_____

_____

_____

At last the show was over. Everybody was safe.

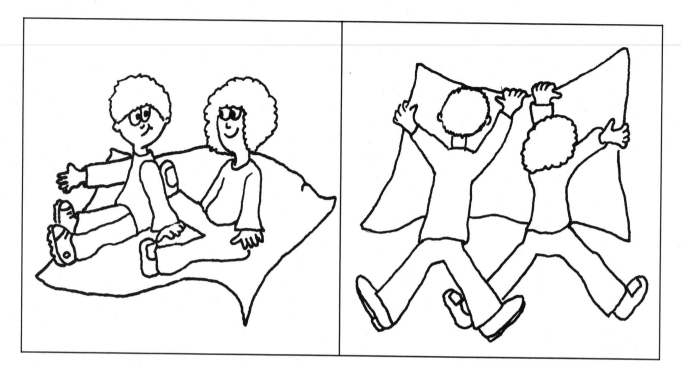

Read the ending of the story about the pictures. Write the beginning and the middle part of the story. Do not forget to write a title.

_____

_____

_____

_____

_____

_____

_____

_____

We landed safely. What a trip!

Read the ending of the story about the picture. Write the beginning and the middle part of the story. Do not forget to write a title.

_____

_____

_____

_____

_____

_____

The witch flew away. Thank goodness that is over with.

Name _____

Date _____

Read the ending of the story about the pictures. Write the beginning and the middle part of the story. Do not forget to write a title.

_____

_____

_____

_____

_____

_____

Finally, they won the dance contest.

GIANT STEPS

Name _____

Date _____

Read the ending of the story about the pictures. Write the beginning and the middle part of the story. Do not forget to write a title.

_____

_____

_____

_____

_____

_____

_____

He could not help but laugh. At least the tennis match was over.

GIANT STEPS

Read the ending of the story about the pictures. Write the beginning and the middle part of the story. Do not forget to write a title.

_____

_____

_____

_____

_____

_____

_____

_____

_____

It was a funny dream — one that I will never forget.

Name _____

Date _____

Read the ending of the story about the picture. Write the beginning and the middle part of the story. Do not forget to write a title.

_____

_____

_____

_____

_____

_____

Soon everyone was happy again.

GIANT STEPS

Read the ending of the story about the pictures. Write the beginning and the middle part of the story. Do not forget to write a title.

_____

_____

_____

_____

_____

_____

After they told each other how they broke their legs, the boys became good friends.

Write a story about the picture. Do not forget the title.

_____

_____

_____

_____

_____

_____

_____

_____

THE BIG PICTURE

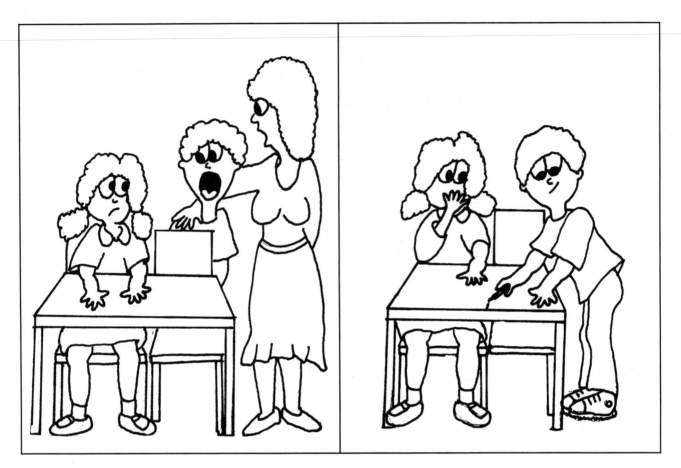

Write a story about the pictures. Do not forget the title.

_____

_____

_____

_____

_____

_____

_____

_____

THE BIG PICTURE

Write a story about the pictures. Do not forget the title.

_____

_____

_____

_____

_____

_____

_____

_____

THE BIG PICTURE

Write a story about the pictures. Do not forget the title.

_____

_____

_____

_____

_____

_____

_____

_____

THE BIG PICTURE

Write a story about the picture. Do not forget the title.

_____

_____

_____

_____

_____

_____

_____

_____

_____

_____

THE BIG PICTURE

Name _____

Date _____

Write a story about the picture.
Do not forget the title.

_____

_____

_____

_____

_____

_____

_____

_____

_____

_____

_____

_____

_____

_____

_____

_____

_____

_____

_____

_____

_____

_____

THE BIG PICTURE

Name _____

Date _____

Write a story about the picture.
Do not forget the title.

_____

_____

_____

_____

_____

_____

_____

_____

_____

_____

_____

_____

_____

_____

_____

_____

_____

THE BIG PICTURE

Name _____

Date _____

Write a story about the pictures. Do not forget the title.

_____

_____

_____

_____

_____

_____

_____

_____

_____

_____